POETS OF QUEENS

edited by
Olena Jennings

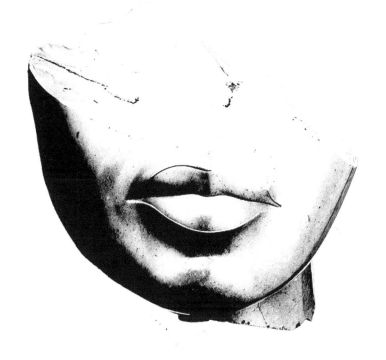

POETS OF QUEENS

edited by
Olena Jennings

Poets of Queens Press
New York, 2020

This anthology is made possible in part by the Queens
Council on the Arts with public funds from the
New York City Department of Cultural Affairs in
partnership with the City Council.

Designed and composed by Oleksandr Fraze-Frazenko.

On the Cover:
Fragment of a Queen's Face ca. 1353–1336 B.C. Egypt.
The MET Collection. The subway photo by Jon Skinner.

ISBN 978-1-7351478-0-2

CONTENTS

FOREWORD

It took me 28 years, but back in 2011 I found myself drawn to New York for a lot of the same reasons I'd been drawn to art and literature throughout my life: the way they celebrate coming from somewhere else and building a nontraditional family; the character of folks you find in New York and the arts – seekers, spiritualists, individualists, big fish from small ponds – people who love life and live it in exquisite ways. Olena Jennings' Poets of Queens is one such family. We gather (often over a meal) once a month with a growing crowd of regulars, and build a common culture together through the sharing of thought and experiences. You'll find in this book great examples of the local flavor of places like Ditmars Boulevard, where each food truck and storefront you pass represents a different corner of the globe and the folks who work there all carry each other's treasures in and out of the Buffalo Exchange. In reading over the poems in this collection again after having heard them first from the authors themselves at Vintage or our appropriate new home, Book Culture LIC, I was struck by how vividly I remember each of them – it's powerful, memorable, quotable work. Thanks a lot for picking up this book. If you haven't yet, please feel free to join us the first Wednesday of the month to enjoy some poetry, some company, and a deeper connection to a very special place.

Penn Genthner

This anthology is a conglomeration of works by poets who participated in the Poets of Queens reading series. For me, they represent my time in Queens, which I began to call home in 2014. These poems also offer a ray of hope in the time we are in now, the COVID-19 crisis that wounded Queens so acutely.

KC Trommer's poem comprehensively addresses the crisis. Some of Wanda Phipps' poems address the personal aspects of the challenging times. One of Maria Lisella's poems addresses the solitude brought on by the pandemic.

The poems as a whole represent the diversity in Queens and the diversity of experience that is necessary to write poems. In these times of racial divide, the poets represent many cultures. Poetry is a unifying force.

The first two readers in the series were Sherese Francis and Lucas Hunt. They read to a packed house that set the series off to a running start.

Later, readers offered a magical diversity, complementing each other with their use of language. Each one brought something different to the stage.

Language itself has been important to the readings. Firas Sulaiman, a Syrian poet, read his poetry in the original Arabic beside his translator, Samantha Kostmayer Sulaiman. Isaac Stackhouse Wheeler read his translations of Russian poetry alongside his own work.

The others in this anthology made an invaluable contribution to literary life in Queens. They include Marissa Anne Ayala, Pichchenda Bao, Rosebud Ben-Oni, Audrey Dimola, Anna O. Dinwoodie, Anna Fridlis, Jared Harél, Emily Hockaday, Safia Jama, Paolo Javier, Ron Kolm, Esther Mathieu, Vijay R. Nathan, Richard Jeffrey Newman, Jackie Sherbow, Sokunthary Svay, Virlana Tkacz, and Micah Zevin.

Olena Jennings

Marissa Anne Ayala

is a writer based in Austin, TX. She earned her BA from Naropa University's Jack Kerouac School of Disembodied Poetics and her MFA in fiction from the New School. Her work has appeared in *Fugue Literary Journal*, *Pen + Brush Literary Magazine*, *Tupelo Press*, *Handwritten*, *Entropy*, *STRATA*, and *Glassworks Magazine*. She was a featured performer with 826NYC, Boundless Tales via Newtown Literary, Poets of Queens, Pen + Brush, Litost, Renegade Reading Series, and attended the Home School Poetry Conference in 2017. She is the founder and Madame of the Austin Poetry Brothel chapter and has poetry forthcoming in The Poetry Society of NY's Poetry Brothel Anthology. Twitter: @MarissaAAyala | Instagram: @poetrybrothel_atx | @marissaanneayala

THIS GIRL

the window is open / she looks westward / cranes her neck for the edges / of field / almost out of view / the field is a grid / a place to graft / a place to meld a version of ocean / of water / of life / slick with

here day is dust / the meadow hot-hued / the indian paintbrush vines / braid / bleed / red onto tall grasses now split & dry & edges scrape / a cyan sky - so empty.

This house is a box / a box to no longer open / a box to only contain / & she / craves-needs-invites / rain as some type of layer / rain as some type of element to wash / clay from the edges of curled paper bubbled on the walls & she reaches / extends towards sky / catches cool / catches wet

dew on the low side of cloud / can we secure night in our fists the way she hides / scraps of tin from the roast / a hen caught / a hen de-feathered / a neck split / a throat enclosed in the the foil / the foil holds the body as is - as was / & she tucks every edge / holds the heat

until aluminum cools & edges scar / burnt / she cuts the edge / curled slips of black ashen tin & it scatters / charred / scarred dark / she jaggedly folds / geometric creases / scrapes index finger & nail across aluminum / unfolds & measures the tightness of the pattern / now complete.

A dollhouse in the corner of room / half-empty / a miniature roast / chicken on its side / rolled onto the floral draped bed in a miniscule grand tiny room / her mother wired lights / *look how the lights turn on* / the house bright in her dim room / the doll inside / the doll stationed / so small by the window / she watches the light

pasted on the wall / just beyond a house / a house that is not a house / just an object to store / just a meal / to not cook / not so different than her own roast / in the oven / downstairs / except that chicken sizzles / and this one / stays preserved

they cannot see / the foil / pasted in the dim corner/ of her room / they cannot see / how she ignites / how she lets light interrupt dark & thinks *I am like the wolves* / like their howls / howls pierce night / pierce through the still / the dim / howls pierce through / the slow burn / of dark while the house sleeps / & she listens to the wind / how it breathes / both with & without her.

THE ARRANGEMENT

Can a stain transform
him standing alone
so unsure of our next arrangement?

In this house of she - a blue mouth emits
particles of noise & light flickers
yellow specks onto his neckline.

The shadow of his hands
dance against a pale wall
& my tongue splinters
& these bones are just glass
beads rotating inside
the house lit
the house waiting

& is it possible to slice color
with a kitchen knife only
to find red bleeds gold?

& is it possible for a kiss
to feel like the sound
of a mandolin high pitched - piercing?

On this road we are hypnotized
by the knowing of buried blue-bells

& you ask, *he bought you a lavender field?*
& I laugh, *no-no*
he brought me to a lavender field &
that field holds so many imprints
of us

& I, I
reshape the laced grass
where soil breaks pockets
of summer wheat

& I, I
dream we ate spoiled
crabapples intoxicated & slurring
mouthfuls of French
in our tree-lit indigo night

& I, I
wash paint onto gneiss pathways
veined & gnarled & dusted
with crumbled schist & all those stone
rainbows pressed together

on this road I paint lavender heart-valves
between sunny yellow lines
on a chemical trail
that carries us elsewhere.

COW'S SKULL: RED, WHITE, & BLUE

At night -
bats devour nectar
& the moon devours heat
cooling the body that lays beneath night's
indigo blanket.

At noon -
hummingbirds devour nectar
& sun devours organs
popping the bubbling cells
& they hiss like steam from that engine.

I stare at this Georgia O'Keefe painting
note how the pink mountains
crumble - dry and cracked -
like her aging skin in that black & white
photo by Stieglitz.

I crave -
O'Keefe's rendition of desert
but know our desert swallows.

I crave -
color. Those thick oil paints that
outline a bleached skull framed in red & blue
- a skull so similar to, but different from, the elk I found
bleached & abandoned in the kitchen
of a torn farm house.

I placed those bones near a hubcap, near a tire,
& asked, won't that melt?

They drove north.
Crossed the desert in a truck.
Huddled in a dim container.
Thoughts on their boy in Texas &
their brother who arranged this crossing.

When the truck stilled
& the temperature rose
the driver unlocked the cargo -
they & they & they
scattered.

This couple ran through night
sunk their boots into cracked earth
ran towards the image of the boy
knowing their brother must look like them-
aged & worried.

Later, they found a faded pink scarf
frayed & clinging
to a flowering cactus.

Brooklyn is so much cooler-
on this wooden bench near the painted Mexican mural
of a woman's naked body
we sip white wine, throw back a beer, or two,
roll cigarettes & smoke
ash falling on the cracked table.

Did you know the mountains are on fire again?

They say when a body disappears
in the desert
vultures scatter limbs
& we face the impossible task to
identify one singular body
from the pink scarf
but there are no singular bodies to restructure.

He ashes the cigarette -

If I could do anything right now,
I would scrape that desert.
Find all the lost bones & carefully put us
back together.

THE KISS OF THE SURREALIST MIND

Lavender wraps her
I am her & she

climbs through a window
into this:

a single cicada's wings expand -

please note the aerodynamic engineering

of her naked body
so expansive -
so part of some lavender field
hidden in the history of this road

& nothing seems to hurt.

He gives me
Earth.
He carves me
Inlets.

(small testimonies of breath)

& one touch is really just a boulder

please note how the vertebrae coils

tied in daisy chains
around & through
the thin of her salt-stained ankles.

He holds her rabid ways on this road &

sage represents the history of blue

&

she doesn't know.

How we contain the sky.

How we contain such tiny heartbeats.

Pichchenda Bao

is an emerging writer and poet. Born at the end of the Khmer Rouge regime in Cambodia, she was an infant when her mother carried her across the border. She and her parents arrived in the United States as refugees. Now she lives, writes, and stays at home, raising her two young children in Long Island City, NY. Her work has been published by *Newtown Literary,* great weather for MEDIA, the Cambodian American Literary Arts Association online zine, and included in *No Tender Fences, An Online Anthology of Immigrant and First-Generation American Poetry,* as well as Queensbound, an audio poetry project curated by KC Trommer. Her work has also been nominated for a Pushcart Prize and made into limited-edition broadsides at the Center for Book Arts. She was an emerging writer fellow at the 2019 Aspen Summer Words conference.

TRESPASS

I was not supposed to be there.
Riding past the corner,
not turning back,
then pause at the top
of what the neighborhood kids called Devil's Hill.
I released the brakes and leaned forward.
The spell of speed and my own power
so enthralling I didn't know
I was not in control.
Until I turned into a tangle
of girl and bike,
crumpled at the bottom.

Someone saw me (a stranger)
came out of their house,
and took me home,
delivering my battered bike and body
to my unwitting parents.

But if I had expected some kind
of stricken sympathy, some gentleness from them,
it would not have been the first time
I was wrong. Their punishment rained down
hard as the sidewalk.

After all, what is a child's flesh wound
to a woman who lost her father to the Khmer Rouge?
What acute injuries are real to a man
who had escaped death multiple times?
And what can a child glean from a love
so complete yet stinging with fear?

My mother had carried me in her arms
through land-mined jungles
to the safety of this wing-clipped childhood.
And I survived to remember
the hot sensation of my righteous anger
closing over me like
                    a newly-formed, tender scab.

I AM NOT YOUR SAFE SPACE

I am not an American,
or so I've been told.
(You speak English so well.)

This isn't about you. It's not personal.
But it is personal.
This is not the first time we've heard this story.
You think you know the ending.
You are wrong.

WHY IS SISYPHUS NOT AN OLD WIVES' TALE?

After all, who came first?
Sisyphus, or me vacuuming a trail
of toddler-scattered Cheerios
from here to the river Styx.

How could I not be the stuff of myth?
My cervix became an oracle.
It dilated to the size of a poppy seed bagel
and released, through a ring of fire,
the future, smelling of animal,
demanding to be fed.

Why did Sisyphus become legend,
then language? His strain, our strain.
His despair, our despair
reflected, refracted, recurring.
We will watch forever
the public sphere men
push up that lonely, dreadful hill.
But no audience for the women,
spinning themselves silly
in domestic circles.
Gears, catching no one's attention.

At least, Sisyphus gets to focus
on just one thing.
My interminable days pile and dissipate
as I wage my foolhardy resistance to entropy.
And no one cares about this denouement:
Olympus and Tartarus are both loose in this world.

ASSIMILATION

I was told in Catholic school, there was only one true faith.
I carried this with me to our dining room table
where platters of whole roasted ducks with
their glossy gold necks curled under, were set out
as offerings to our ancestors.
Ritual without the trappings of church.
I did not understand the words my father spoke –
the three Buddhist invocations.
Instead, I watched the incense's burning tip,
a red-hot blasphemy in passage
down to my father's prayered hands,
waiting for that pillar of ash to fall.
There was a makeshift altar
with the few surviving photographs
of our dead, and there, my mother placed
a full plate of food for ghosts.
I did not know what to believe.

In Catholic school, I was taught that God
could only fit inside a pristine mouth.
I was zealous in the way only a child can be
when given a set of unassailable rules.
I spoke in perfect English until even my name became a tiresome translation.
How could I have known that I would be forever altered?
That my tongue would harden into a muscle memory of rejection?

This is not a penance.
See how I instruct my young children:
       Turn to your grandparents.
       Press your palms together.
       Raise them to your forehead,
       Repeat after me.
       Sahtook, Mah Yeh.
       Sahtook Puk Tha.
Amen, Grandmother.
Amen, Grandfather.
Amen, blessing and greeting.
Amen, the glee that bursts from my parents every time,
though their grandchildren's tongues are still unpracticed and awkward.
Amen, this daily communion of the living and the dying.

ODE TO THE BOX OF DISCARDED POWER CORDS

I should get rid of you.
Take your jumble
on a subway ride
to one of those recycling events
the city hosts for those of us
who need help letting go.
Your labyrinth of un-use,
disuse, refuse waits
under the bed. Every day,
you gather dust
to your loose coils.
Soft wisps of indeterminate
gray held together by what?
Static electricity? The
unrelenting attraction
of matter to matter?
I don't even know
where you'd fit.
Your potential lies
vacant inside.
Who remembers what power
you were meant to bring?

Rosebud Ben-Oni

is the winner of the 2019 Alice James Award for *If This Is the Age We End Discovery*, forthcoming in 2021, and the author of turn around, *BRXGHT XYXS* (Get Fresh Books, 2019). She is a recipient of fellowships from the New York Foundation for the Arts (NYFA) and CantoMundo. Her work appears in *POETRY, The American Poetry Review, POETS.org, The Poetry Review (UK), Tin House, Guernica, Black Warrior Review, Prairie Schooner, Electric Literature's Recommended Reading, TriQuarterly, Hayden's Ferry Review, The Journal, Hunger Mountain, The Adroit Journal, The Southeast Review, North American Review, Salamander, Poetry Northwest*, among others. Her poem "Poet Wrestling with Angels in the Dark" was commissioned by the National September 11 Memorial & Museum in New York City, and published by The *Kenyon Review Online*. She writes for *The Kenyon Reviewblog*. She is currently editing a special chemistry poetry portfolio for Pleiades, and is finishing a series called The Atomic Sonnets, in honor of the
Periodic Table's 150th Birthday. Find her at 7TrainLove.org

POET WRESTLING WITH GRAVITON AS {{ :: *GRAVITRON* :: }}

I created you {*exo*}. From origins {*tender*} & unproven. For you.
I crossed the streams & struck. Incurable. Fire
left ::
unguarded

& {untendered} desire. For you alone. I swallowed.
Organic mercury. Nitro. Unripened.
Neutron. Stars. I burst. & bled.
A people. From your exo-particle.
Veins. & vessels. Fallen. Of faithful

exodus.
No one can {ever} leave
behind. Memory. Is not survival.

But a shrill {*exotoxin*}. Veil &. Cry.

{*of desperate moons*}

spinning. Into darkness.
& I tell myself I'm indelicate planet.
Who'd rather hydrogen bomb
the :: *exordium* :: of my own
canon. Unlike you. My son. My

{!{ :: *Gravitron* :: }!}

I changed
one thing. From original quantum. & won't say
its name. Since the exoteric makes. Exotsis
& creates both the snake. & the garden.
My sweet. Havoc. Of harbors.
Expose this
World ::

as coded & skin-deep.
From the other side

:: {*of the screen*} ::

they so sorely want
    to breach

        when nothing can hold
        their *{bonfires &}* fields

         :: {within me} ::

when I'm the last I'll get it
the worst it's nothing
{I didn't foresee}

      just so you could leave my loving

        seams a little better
          off a little
           less

      {:: xo ::}

LOVE SONG #3: TO ISABELLE & DAN

—Written for the New York Botanical
Valentine's Day Programming,
February 11th, 2018

—& speaking of excuses, dear Isabelle,

what do you have to say of all your accumulated lateness
        since that first fateful date that almost
                wasn't, like the best

song are by bands you didn't know in the first place & won't
        remember, only an excuse
                to keep someone
                        waiting, as in someone
                                you haven't even yet met, & speaking

of lateness— I've lost my train
        of thought because this poem keeps getting interrupted.
                That, however, is *not* an excuse— very late
                        garden-goers keep stopping

by my table. Not for poems but directions
        to the chocolate station. There's half an hour left
                until the garden closes & really, who can blame
                them? I don't know
                        how bitter beans become sweet & I don't
                        take their Valentine's

day preferences personally. Just like your "very strong
        interest," Isabelle, in Steve Buscemi.

("Give it time," Dan rubs his face,
        the most hopeful declaration of love
                I've heard today.) —& I guess time does reveal all

we don't remember, what we use
        as excuses, the greyest

of dances, Dan might say. Like perhaps Steve Buscemi *was* considered

for *Fifty Shades.* But then again, Isabel would remember.
Or would she? You two are the last poem

I'll write here today, in this garden of aquatic plants & halfway
to cocoa bean heaven & you probably won't remember
if I tell you that I too am perpetually late

& this evening is no excuse either to ponder,
Dan, just what is that Stevie song about New

Year's Day & April Rain. (Not Buscemi but Wonder.)
I'm pretty sure I know the title,
since it *was* playing when you asked

about "that song of months," but such an answer
comes too easy, didn't it? Must be something more
elusive. Or rather: in the spirit of love, you were trying
to *not* remember. & I'm still working out
my own excuses

for missing my stop. Say my train losing itself in February rain
it thought April. & how some trains forget their own
rails. How they'd rather stride & misstep. Yes,
hours later I'll say it won't happen again.
No, it will not won't.
Promise.

Audrey Dimola

is a Bearer of Legend, alchemical artist and poet, event curator, sacred space-holder, youth mentor, and impassioned advocate for education, access, and understanding of the healing interrelation of myth, mental health, and the ecologies of spirit. She has self-published 4 books including "WILDLIGHT" and "THE BOOK OF LEGEND," performed in venues both intimate and massive around NYC including The Cathedral of Saint John the Divine, LaGuardia Performing Arts Center, and Brooklyn Museum, and has nearly a decade of experience curating and hosting countless multidisciplinary arts events (including the first ever Queens Literary Town Hall in 2013) and working creatively in diverse communities. She is also proud to serve her community as Director of Public Programs at Long Island City's wondrous outdoor art-space, Socrates Sculpture Park. Join her adventures online: audreydimola.com / IG: audreydimola

THE BODY IS A PRAYER FOR BEGINNING

"many of us spend our whole lives running from feeling with the mistaken belief that you cannot bear the pain. but you have already borne the pain. what you have not done is feel all you are beyond the pain." -- st. bartholomew.

the body is a spell
conjured in tandem by god + god self
for the truth of life.

they say god went native in the incarnation
when you kneel by the river
you praise
to your own blood flowing

the yorubans say
prostration really means to be still
in the face of the storm
and my body is relearning to get low to the ground
to hear the truth encoded in the sacred inside itself.

what are the things i have survived?
punishing myself with negligence for nourishment
bad food and badder love
my obsession is the fractals of my self reflection
the first time i really looked in the mirror and talked to myself
i cried.

the body is a prayer for beginning
sometimes a graveyard sometimes a deathscape sometimes a
reliquary i wrote to hold all the stories about the ghosts
their names scrawled on my ribs and sewn through my heart
i couldn't wait to find the eternal man to complete my
completion, my god
all the knowledge that comes after what we think is the fall
i thank god for her. i thank god for eve
her expulsion from the garden her seeming betrayal gave birth
to the wilderness inside ourselves
inside me,
i realize now the great bridge between the worlds i couldn't stop

visioning leaping from to end my life BROUGHT the end of my
life, even as i stand before you here,
the end of the body of falsehood
the body is prayer for the end of falsehood
and the resurrection of everything i could remember
and everything i hadn't yet created--
as Me.

* *

i want to invite us all-- into prayer
even if you have never prayed even if you have never sought god
or source energy
she is a sacred tether leading us back to ourselves stuck with
knots that only our small stubborn hands can undo.

what is a futuring action?
what is the future the body is walking into by virtue of its
existence
by virtue of its will to continue onward, here
to cry and scream and dance and sing and pray
for the recollection of the goodness
for the recollection of the god inside us all

* *

i walked into a random church the other day just outside grand central
its doors had great golden lions roaring on the handles dotted
with the drops of earlier rain and i knelt before the statue of the
sacred heart
the stillness inside the wonder inside the shaking strangeness
inside the resolute
jesus was a legend was a prophet was a parable was a mortal
man was an echo
i see him as my brother in arms, closer than some distant avatar
and in my own way instead of closing my eyes and bowing my head i
outstretched my arms
showing him the holes
in my own hands
bleeding the knowing that

the body is a prayer for beginning
the body bears a gift inside a wound, a wound inside a gift
32

and it is UP TO US to not forsake it
it is UP TO US to stand honestly within it
for however we are anguished or grievous, joyous or afraid
there is only one moment and it is FOREVER
this body this hope this willingness to say

i love you
i forgive you
i am not broken
i am still brave
i love you
i forgive you
i am not broken
i am still brave

i love you
i forgive you
this is a prayer for beginning
to walk Forward
in my own way
and it begins with YOU
and with me
every single day.

* * *

i only have these small shining moments here with you.
feeling my way up, blind, this endless staircase
met at every single landing by the spectres of falsehood that
nearly claimed my life
the voices now so familiar
as if laced inside my blood

you are mentally ill
you are a monster
you bring destruction
to everyone you touch
your life is pointless
your work is worthless
you will never be free
you will never be enough
you are beyond hope

33

you are beyond help
there is nothing in the cosmos
to hear your lamentations
you are lost
and you will never find your way
Home.

in the darkness i can see a tiny flickering light
far in the distance further along up high on the staircase
a little girl is whispering so faintly
underneath the constant thrum of the voices, the shadows, their
purrs and their snarls
she seems exhaustively above me, utterly unreachable, but i can
hear her
not with my ears but inside me

* * *

i love you
i forgive you
i am not broken
i am still brave
i love you
i forgive you
i am not broken
i am still brave

* * *

there is a propulsion
in the incantation
and in the infinite time
inside many mortal years
her voice becomes louder
more perceptible than the others
more present than those
who never stop talking
who never stop damning
pleading, grasping, treacherously
being
and one day
after you have put down your sword
and

unclenched your jaw along with your fists
you will find yourself
standing before her
her bright face just barely illuminated
by that one small flame
and after turning around to look down
at the staircase you have devoted your life to climbing
and up to the overwhelming height you still have yet to traverse
she takes your hand and
presses your palm to the wall
and without a sound it falls away
all of it
the narrow staircase
the darkness
the voices
that feeling of
utter
worthlessness
loneliness
the linearity
the bottomed out gut burning scarcity
of climbing and climbing and
never getting any farther or higher or closer

**

and you are blind this time by the light instead of the darkness.
the spaciousness regained inside your consciousness
the steady power of the prayer still repeating, growing the
golden fields before you-- the waterfalls and the flowers, the
thunder atop the mountains in the distance, the shimmering
deserts and teeming forests, the sun on your face, the simplicity
of that.
warmth.

your eyes adjust to the softness of the focus
and recognize yourself in the little girl before you
and for the first time in so many years
you feel back inside your body
you feel safe
you feel daringly open-ended
and like you've made it
really, created it--
the way back
Home.

* * *

remember to make your own prayers
remember that your own prayers exist all the time inside you
maybe just in the slightness of a whisper
or a dancing candle-wick
or the gentle push that gives way
from that suffocating staircase
from the endless pointless
uncertainty of it all
to precious words and gestures of
small at first but
furiously future-making
bright and
light-shaping
HOPE--
that love and forgiveness and
wondrous
imagining
flowing out
and tapped in
from our bodies
to expansivity for
True Life.

may we say thank you to our bodies.
may we say thank you to ourSelves.
AHO.

Anna O. Dinwoodie

was born in Berkeley, California and grew up on a hill. A degree in cultural anthropology and a desire to see other places have left her fascinated by intersections of landscape, belief, and words. In addition to writing poetry, she is an editor and German-English translator, and feeds her soul by dancing, walking in the woods, and drinking tea. Anna is currently pursuing an MFA in Creative Writing & Literary Translation at Queens College.

LETTER FROM A FAR FRIEND

Empty, I am like the shell left behind by a sea creature searching for a better home. The growing, the moving on, happened to somebody else – to everyone else – and left me here the ghost of a life sitting on wet sand. Floating now, ready to be pulled away by the tongues of tides I cannot withstand, loosened from all ties to life and the living –
soon to be gone.

Maybe your letter can tide me over here for another day, the loops of your sometimes-cursive letters keep me moored, like rays of sudden sun embodied in dust motes, tie me to some solid shore. Maybe the practice of writing can tether me, the footprints of my pen produce a physical bond between me and this page, and this table, this life, remnant shell of a former –

My father's first tendance to hit me.
The untriumphant return of the parental dependent.
And you: slow sinking into a sand pit big enough to swallow two, a shared world suddenly vanished.

Not traceless though; the traces lie everywhere.

The rope I wanted you to bind me with.
The words I am maybe most grateful for:

I know you're sensitive, Anna.
It's one of your best qualities.

And now, just there I feel
the taughtening.

Those words the ones that tie me to a shore I can no longer see. Words that remember the best of me: unchangeable essence often overlooked, buried in sand cast by friends, family, and strangers alike –

You think too much;
Don't dwell on it;
Pretend you do not see, think, feel, speak, hear –

here,

here is the rope,

not lost to sea after all. It binds me to something below
sand, deeper than bedrock, some immutable force at the core of
what it is to live. In my essence, I sense; this quality of the living
uniquely mine. One of my best; and from here, if I follow this
line, my hands on this strand, maybe
I will find the others.

LET LOOSE ENDS GO
(Goodbye)

I wanted to feel through your fingers.
Your hands firm and slender,
they could hold me well.
Could stroke my hair,
my cheek,
my thigh,
my

I wanted to bite your lip gently.
Your kisses were tame,
so sweet, they left my lips
salty.

The secret I wanted,
the textbook affair:
poem slipped into pocket,
back pressed against stair:
want arching brows and sliding eyes,
want arching backs and sliding thighs,
want openings
and closings,
your lips on
omissions,
your hands on
the backs of
my thighs,
eyes
close
lose
clothes
legs
lock
drum
nock
bow
thrum —

Sing my skin to sleep.

It is not for nothing
that I long

To turn the world to words
and words to world.

I wanted other memories
to offer the ghosts
of my lost.

Release
from my thoughts.

A throated sound
of skin untamed
where pain and pleasure
are the same
where lips have roots
and air cadence
where world is breathed
into being
every moment
just
once.

PROWL

For I want to devour a man,
So I have tiger eyes.
I want to harm and hold a man;
I have salving canines.

I long to taste his tongue
With my teeth,
Sink into his arms
With my claws,
Lick blood from his lips,
Sunscreen skinflakes,
A dead-cell taste
Like hunger
Like plunder
Like devour
Like scratch and bite
Like kiss and fight
Like match and light
Like prey and flight
Like noon at night,
Your flesh my rite.

Sherese Francis

is a Queens-based poet, editor, text artist, workshop facilitator, and literary curator of the mobile library project, J. Expressions. She has published work in journals and anthologies including *Furious Flower, Obsidian Literary, The Operating System, Cosmonauts Avenue, No Dear, Apex Magazine, La Pluma Y La Tinta's New Voices Anthology, The Pierian Literary Review, Bone Bouquet, African Voices, Newtown Literary, and Free Verse.* Additionally, she has published two chapbooks, *Lucy's Bone Scrolls* and *Variations on Sett/ling Seed/ling.* In 2020, she was named a finalist in the Furious Flower Poetry Prize. Sherese is currently an editor for Harlequin Creature. To find out more about her work, visit futuristicallyancient.com.

HISTORY AND THE PRESENT INVADE EACH OTHER'S SPACE

72.111 miles = Discovering mobility *1.2 miles* art gasping for air, thirsting for water. A new moon brings *9.5 miles* a harvest of words birthed from a Zong ship. I chose the lie of comfort in a faster *11.3 miles* train ride.Who am I *3.6 miles* if I think I am tired of old words and want to exhale a new thought? Should I have followed my intuition *1.8 miles* instead of missing the earlier train and arriving late to "it can happen here?" Emptied my hands *1.8 miles* of golden nuggets and headed out to dip my hands in curry sauce. How do I grow *1.5 miles* love letters to a shifting home I am now starting to recognize as mine. Stepping on the rolled dice of acorns: choosing whether to take the straight path *1.5 miles* or walk crooked to avoid passing by unwanted men. A firehouse cannot cool the rage caused by whiteness; rage I am tired of; *13 miles* rage with no answers. Hunting around to fulfill my hunger before I enter *2.1 miles* a house of hounds with warning words in their mouths. A hovering presence: a large figure dressed in red wakes my awareness; *12.3 miles* I pulled out my keys and took the end seat. Tracking human flow *1.8 miles* through the installation of light and water. I have no sure words to offer for a plan flowing *0.3 miles* together around me. Going against the usual choice of how I mangle *.011 miles* death in my body. Picking up an incendiary art *0.4 miles* in a house of books. Looking for dirt and a clay pot for an unknown *0.3 miles* plant. Walking through a hidden passageway *1.3 miles* in the middle of a street to avoid the attention of unwanted men. How do I inspire ink: *1 mile* bind it in time? I am asked why I begin *1 mile* my work at the end. How do I travel *3.2 miles* to the child within me who feels so much of the world, and yet experienced so little of it? Contemplating the dark violet bruise flowering *3.2 miles* into unheard language and stops in-between for nourishment.

NEW PORTS TRIPTYCH: I CARRY A RAPTURE AROUND MYSELF

CAR Through Sub Nu/Alts
I took the E train
read the plug
into a packet of New Ports
seeded next to me
an I am is
carried into this body
read as divine escape
when the world feels
to   Moses
draw out the wandering between
choices and vices
breaking points
part the way to an unheard
begging to be transported
in the mouth
the nowhere called paradise
the tree of knowing desire lets fall
a wand of magic and makes it sacred
resting in your breath

SMK

the leaves are calling
Ci Ci Ci Ci Ci
Ga Ga Ga Ga Ga
Ci Ci Ci Ci Ci
Ga Ga Ga Ga Ga
lie in the couch   err
the burning fly away
lie in the trans/see/dive bod
lie in the expected object
a word thrown directly across
flickering into your ears
some unseen sound
calling you outside
crick crack crick crack
crackling into enlightenment
cackling into a foreign attraction
the rolling of verbs
the gears turning
ad diction   towards potential
medicinal leavings
smearing it all over
into some sliver of sight
the twist to return
see broken selves
and place all of You
together again
into a form of vic   tory

LIRR

this is your receipt:	and is (k)not	a ticket for travel:
like a king named lear	learn the lure	the liar in a lore
the lair of a lie	need a light?	a ligature of logos
a sea of soul	drain the chrism	a tree's reincarnation
the real/road	to a longing	a mouthful of words
be a why	as the one	vapor hovering around
lie down	find the tracks	in the tricks made
wonder at sense	sniff out some	lesson received
something else	lurking in a vehicle	horns let slip
what kind	tricks are you	training the body
small wonders will	between teeth	piping language that
call you back	calling you back	called you back

A FACT OF RUINS
(QUESTIONING BONES AT THE AFRICAN BURIAL GROUND)

Who buried you?
Human nature builds nations on a monstrous crucifixion.

What killed you?
A riddle is a question forced between a living image and
strangulation of what could have been.

Where is your head looking?
The vein still throbs in the ring finger of my phantom arm
stretching across the Atlantic.

When did you breathe your last breath?
My ribs married dirt and my breath became a pearl shut within
its clam.

Why is there a circle of bricks on your legs?
Institutions are dried up memories of fugitivity, constructing
burial mounds on the waves of legs.

Anna Fridlis

started writing to deal with the confusion and stress of
immigration from Astrakhan, Russia to Northern Virginia as a
tween in the mid 90s. Her current writing practice spans poetry
and non-fiction, with a focus on how family history and trauma
wind with larger political and cultural contexts. Anna received
the New School Creative Writing MFA Program's chapbook prize
for nonfiction for The Edge of the Known World, a memoir in
progress, upon graduation. She has since been teaching writing
at Parsons The New School for Design with occasional stints in
other local universities. Anna serves as contributing editor at
the literary and arts organization The Seventh Wave and is a
freelance writer, editor, and writing coach. She lives in Jersey
City and enjoys walking through forests, photography, drawing,
and taking care of her plants.

I. ON THE PHENOMENOLOGY OF MY BODY THROUGH TIME

At first—the invisibility of the body,
Then— the wonder of the body,
Then— the shame of the body,
Then— the rupture of the body,
The dissolution of the body,
Its trembling stasis,
Its reconfiguration,
Its tentative desire to exist again,
Its desperate desire to want to.

II. 3 HAIKU

I'm writing a poem,
eyelash against collarbone
fluttering Morse code.

***

The trouble with me
is thought equals action, the
imagined is real.

***

Night, my face buried
in his side, I keep saving
myself in others.

III. HAIKU DIPTYCH:
Art in the Age of Mechanical Reproduction, Transposed

Art in the Age of
Mechanical Reproduc-
tion, C sharp minor.

Soviet children re-
citing poetry on chairs
ad infinitim.

IV. RESPONSIBILITY TO THE DEAD AND DYING

I do not feel bitterness
Toward my mother
Anymore.
I have forgotten, let myself forget
Rage I owe my-then-self.
Is this betrayal?
Or am I
Maturing,
Like they all said?

*

Survivor's guilt affects those who've lived beyond
Disaster, watched
Flesh of their flesh
Bone of their bone
Blood of their blood
Melt away at their side,
Like Adam robbed of rib—
But look what sprang of it— his wife,
His love, to be at his side and of it.
She took his life, a piece of it anyway, and lived—absorbed it into
Gristle, joint, sinew, muscle,
The soft folds that house
Sprung bone.

*

What have I taken of the girl I was, when all she asked was voice, mine,
For her use?
There was a day I chose happiness over truth, I remember it like it was
Today.
I said to my-then-self, I said, just stop, enough, of probing, parsing,
Analyzing, even
Though that was all my-then-self knew and was
Because there had not been a choice until
That day, not really.

*

It had to do with weightlessness, fleshlessness,
a thinning out of marrow;
I used it all up to get to a deeper understanding, I
was paying it forward with flesh and strength; if I was
transparent, the world would be more visible; I could see
right through my belly into its blood.

*

Then my-then-self said, stop this! I am disappearing I am
Nearly gone, eaten up by wakefulness, I want my
Flesh back, to be
Human again and see less,
Less of the time.

*

I don't feel bitterness
Toward my mother
Anymore.

*

My first flesh was hers. But that's not really
Why. It is just over. It's just
The end of my-then-self
That's sending up its last rasping cry to be remembered,
Because she did not have enough
Love to eat then and wasted away.
The only thing she asked, my-then-self,
Was to keep her shadow with me, for all time, to write her into
Eternity because she always knew
She would not last.

Jared Harél

is the author of the debut poetry collection, *Go Because I Love You* (Diode Editions, 2018). He's been awarded the 'Stanley Kunitz Memorial Prize' from *American Poetry Review*, the 'William Matthews Poetry Prize' from *Asheville Poetry Review*, and two 'Artist Grants' from Queens Council on the Arts. His poems have appeared in such journals as *APR*, *Arts & Letters*, *Harvard Review*, *Newtown Literary*, *Ploughshares*, *Poetry Daily*, *Threepenny Review* and *Tin House*. Harél is a drummer, teaches writing at Nassau Community College and lives in Rego Park, NY with his wife and two kids.

LATE-OCTOBER AT WASHINGTON IRVING'S HOUSE
(Tarrytown, NY)

There is rain and there is *rain*
and this is the latter.
It lays upon us heavy and cold

as we scramble up the pathway
to the dead author's home.
My daughter, undeterred, dashes ahead

past splayed sycamores
and a plastic skeleton roped
to a post. She pines only

for hot cider, Halloween-themed
desserts—is well-versed in the economy
of obstacle and reward.

But my son, too toddler to know
this will pass, presses his soaked face
against my shoulder.

He chokeholds my neck
as though the rumble of dark hooves
still trouble these woods,

which they do, in a way, gaining
on us even. But not before
our cider. Not before sweets.

THE BURBS
(for Dan)

Housewarming wine tight in my grip,
I compliment the molding,
your natural light. I push away
the twelve exits on the expressway
between us – this widening
of space – to praise all
you've refurbished or replaced.
While our kids clobber each other
with clumps of bubble-wrap, we head up
to view bedrooms, a third bath,
an attic which requires we duck and rise
as through a sacred tomb—
a next level in some videogame
we'd cut school to play.
And though this feels like a future
we agreed to flee while smoking weed
in the Bagel Boss parking-lot
or heaving three-pointers
at the local Y, you seem pleased
with the counterspace,
the fireplace and full-acre yard.
Neighbors wave from the brightness
of their patios as I loosen
my fingers; surrender
the wine. Downstairs, our kids
have annexed the Home Depot boxes—
built foxholes and tunnels
to ride out the night.

MY STUPID PRIDE

is hard and rusted
as a lug nut—

brownish-red speckles
eating into steel

stripped of its grooves;
I haven't a clue

how to tug it loose,
how to unscrew

this thing I drilled in
so tightly, back

when I swore it
would never undo me.

WOMAN WATCHING A MOVIE ON HER iPHONE
WHILE SITTING FRONT-ROW AT MY POETRY READING

At first glance, I believe she's asleep:
head bowed, shoulders still. Then I spot

that flat, flickering screen; twin wires
twisting up her torso to neat

earbuds embedded in her skull.
She has chaperoned, it seems, an aunt

or mother – older woman with walker –
to this evening event. An act

of devotion, though her benevolence
ends there. She is wearing

a red sweater. Her dark hair
whips into a bun. Clearly, she doesn't care

if there is news in poetry, or if rabid hounds
rip through the hall. She hears nothing

against her will, and fair enough.
Life is hard and television is fantastic.

Yet afterwards, I want desperately
to ask what she was watching,

is it worth checking out? But she is
busy guiding that woman

with the walker, eyes on the ground
to ensure she doesn't trip.

Emily Hockaday

is the author of *Space on Earth, Ophelia: A Botanist's Guide, What We Love & Will Not Give Up,* and *Starting a Life,* as well as the forthcoming *Beach Vocabulary* from Red Bird Chaps. Her poems have appeared in a number of journals, most recently *Parks & Points, Coffin Bell,* and *Gaze.* She is the managing editor of *Analog Science Fiction & Fact* and *Asimov's Science Fiction,* and along with Jackie Sherbow coedited the horror anthology *Terror at the Crossroads.* She can be found on the web at www.emilyhockaday.com and @E_Hockaday.

VERNAL POOL

My own body served
as the safe haven; free
of predators, seasonal,
a thing that might
dry up in the coming months.
The little life I was incubating
couldn't know what awaited me.
An all-consuming fear,
the vacant look
of a town gone dark,
a need bigger than the crater
that loss left. I know
of no spring to tap.

SALTWATER COMPONENTS

After the hurricane broke through the sandy path,
the freshwater marsh became saltwater, an ecosystem changing
in moments. What it meant was more shore for terrapins
to dig divots and deposit their eggs, more room
for horseshoe crab mating. I have stood at
the broken edge of the path and contemplated the bay
and the reedy islands I see from landing and departing
planes. It is easy to float. It is status quo to keep
above water. When did it become so enticing
to make a different choice? The tide goes out,
and remnants of aquatic life are left, scattered
in pieces along the wet—but quickly drying—sand.

COME SPRING

Overnight, a cannon sounds:
a crack across the frozen pond.
It was here my father became
supernatural. Like the fish trapped
within the thick ice,
he knew how to become
dormant, to feign death.
Beneath the ice of Black Pond,
the eyes looking out aren't the lidless
orbs of sunfish and stripers. I recognize
the faces. I need only wait for a thaw.

THE GHOST

The family is blaming me again
for the aches and pains that come with growing,
for the clouds that hold low against
their brick apartment building,
even for the love that moves through
their blood vessels like snakes.
The woman holds her daughter with equal measure
love and fear. It is hard for her
to distinguish one feeling from another,
and as she rests her sinuses
over her herbal tea, she thinks of me.
I perceive the word ghost behind her teeth.
At night when the parents sleep, I move
his hand to her arm, I slide a foot against
a foot. I whisper: you are safe, you are safe,
you are safe, for now, in her ear the whole night through.

FORGET ABOUT THE GHOST

The air gets warmer,
and the ghost diminishes.
Sometimes I catch the ghost
in the corner of my eye, but I never see it
straight on. Have I ever actually seen
the ghost? My baby is almost two,
and she has a word for everything.
A leaf is a tree. At least that's what she tells me.
Almost, I say.

If she's ever seen the spiky green shoots of crocus
exiting the earth, she won't remember. I repeat the word
crocus until it feels like it has no meaning.
Spring is just days away; the woods are full of sand,
the color hasn't come yet. As if carried on the wind,
green will appear in dots, then waves
of tiny leaves unfurling. My daughter will learn
to love this season and it's impossible optimism.
It may be that she will forget about the ghost,
until one day perhaps she is a mother herself,
watching her own child, feeling something
just over her shoulder.

Lucas Hunt

is a celebrated American poet and the president of HUNT
Auctioneers, who was born and raised in rural Iowa. His work
has been published in The New York Times, and received
The John Steinbeck Award for Poetry.

FATHER DEMO

In April pigeons peck the rain-wet square
and Japanese Zelkovas bloom chartreuse,
first dates resume, pizza in the piazza,
guys from the neighborhood work something out,
newspapers, dogs and salads reappear—
Our Lady of Pompeii is here to stay
another twenty years, once photographs
were printed out to share with friends, print doubles
we would say, drunk in the shade, youthful, free
as pigeons skirted fountain lips a priest
claimed there's no dilemma to great for time
to heal, inactive or involved, we sit
together on benches of future shock,
survivors one and all from foreign lands.

GEORGE'S SANDWICHES

Of all the things to see or touch in Midtown
I keep returning to the sandwich story,
not Campbell Apartment, pop-up Tiffany's
or cosmic turquoise painted ceiling,
(although I'm mad about commercial glory
and sculpture bursting pediment).
It goes like this, there was a young man who
took vows of poverty and every night
Grand Central station became his foundation—
George handed sandwiches to homeless people
and listened to their cares, he started there,
anyone who is generous will tell
you that change starts somewhere, it continues
beyond the sandwich but I'm late to work.

CIUDAD NUEVA

A water fountain plumes for us to taste
moments together only last so long,
remember the High Line's mile long opera,
it seemed to take many hours to find
our way, the new city arose from trains,
Hudson Yards never had a care now gobs
of people stroll there, Vessel twisting dreams
outside the Shed and images of Spain,
enough to do to sell the lot at auction,
experience supreme, for all the world
to come and see our amplified conclusion,
manmade attractions taking center stage,
the highest outdoor skydeck in the West
surveys New Jersey, from ashes come wings.

STOP AND SMELL THE HORSES

Once upon The Oak Bar we drank martinis
and heard a horse drawn carriage jingle
The Plaza steps, before Central Park South
became a billionaire's row I napped
off a hangover, far from used booksellers
who make Grand Army continental,
and gala goers marched along stone walls
laid by hand, many moons ago—
now city planners frame the land with steel
beyond imagination, who can guess
what supertall skyscrapers shall predict,
remembering my afternoon siesta
before The Jitney home, heartbreak express,
or baseball game with friends at summer's end.

THE BRIGHT FLOW

Tonight may be the best night of your life
on stage before a rowdy crowd,
Manhattan skyline, river flowing strong,
a massive tent protects us from the rain
as Mayor Bloomberg welcomes donors back
to Pier Two for another black tie ball—
tradition errors, innovation wins,
our parks are places for the past to grow
into things better, tidal estuaries
receive the ocean's gift of absolution,
kids learn about the land and architecture
before it is too late. Will we destroy
our home for further profit and extinct?
Just as you stood to see the sun, we stood.

Safia Jama

was born to a Somali father and an Irish American mother in Queens, New York. A Cave Canem graduate fellow, she has published poetry in *Ploughshares*, *RHINO*, *Cagibi*, *Boston Review*, *Spoken Black Girl*, and *No Dear*. Her poetry has also been featured on WNYC's *Morning Edition* and CUNY TV's *Shades of US* series. Jama is the author of *Notes on Resilience*, which was selected for the New-Generation African Poets chapbook box set series, edited by Kwame Dawes and Chris Abani (*Akashic Books 2020*).

THE LONG BOND

My dad is the only Somali on Cape Cod
and can't pronounce his *p*'s.

His English is otherwise excellent.

"Say Long Pond," we say.
"Long Bond," he says.

"Shall we go to the beach, or the pond?" we ask.
"I prefer the bond," he says.

I prefer the bond too, Dad.

Sandy pines
surround the beach in a ring

and teenage jailers watch
you swim getting fresh water

up your nose
and needles stab

between your wet toes
all the way home.

3AM

I wake to a throat full of crows.

Lightning and melodrama,
followed by a ten-year drizzle.

The crops don't care
to hear the story—

I left you
my lucky bamboo on the sill.

In the fridge
a cupful of blood.

ODE TO A PROBIOTIC GUMMY BEAR

Gummy bear with benefits,
for three days in a row,
I've had the bowels
of an 8-year-old.

You, Gummy, are alive.

You wear sugar like
dreamy body glitter.

Waiting on line at Rite Aid,
a Gerber-fat baby
reached out a hand.

I smiled and said,
"These aren't for you."

If you never disappoint me,
I won't judge
you for being generic.

You are a bionic gummy:
one of your ears, collapsed.

I eat the maximum suggested number.

A gentle but firm parameter:
Chew two to four gummies daily.

You look like a little embryo
in the palm of my hand.

What are you holding so tightly?

WATERCOLORS

It's raining and Grandma's painting a beach scene.

She lets me try a little line,
and I let loose the breakers down by Breakwater Road,
frightening
          her little flock
    of floating *m*'s.

"That's enough," she says
her frame gone rigid,
her weak heart quickening.

Restless, I go to the parlor organ
to tap out low-key melodies
in a minor key.

The music attracts my mother, who requests
"Nobody Knows the Trouble I've Seen."

She sings along weakly, her voice fraying at each *seen.*

Later, I wander to the La-Z-Boy
to visit my grandfather's ghost.

He sips oxygen, ten years sober
on earth, and ten in heaven.

I hear a voice say, "Ah, that Cape Cod
air puts you right to sleep!"

WISH FOR A SAILBOAT IN THE UPSIDE DOWN SEA

I want a far slice of your champagne cake,
that piece you always hide from me.

A few pink coral trees, all fetchingly lace.

Two centuries pass, and your cake riches
layer upon layer of iced frosting
dotted with sugar spheres
hewn in the rougher parts.

Softer shells mimic tiny ears
while sea urchins patrol
cooling pans of sand.

A galley of green weeds stay (or go)
out of respect for your quiet bones
while clown-fish lend levity,
waxing poetic.

The starfish sew on buttons,
lobbying always for stars and star-shapes
in a muted kind of lemon cream.

I long to dwell deep in your velvet corals
extending up and up:

God-fingers always after
unreachable light
that filigrees the sea in strands of sweet
gold leaf—edible, of course.

I dream and drift with the dead
promise of dead seas
and you,
somehow still dancing
with your imaginary umbrella,
little boat,
turning and turning
in your last best coat.

Paolo Javier

The former Queens Borough Poet Laureate (2010-2014), he was born in the Philippines and grew up in Las Piñas, Metro Manila; Katonah, Westchester County; El-Ma'adi, Cairo; Burnaby and North Delta, Metro Vancouver. He's produced three albums of sound poetry with Listening Center (David Mason), including the limited edition pamphlet/cassette Ur'lyeh/ Aklopolis and the booklet/cassette Maybe the Sweet Honey Pours, and was a featured artist in Greater NY 2015 and Queens International 2018: Volumes. He recently completed his fifth full-length book of poetry, OBB, a (weird postcolonial techno dreampop) comics poem forthcoming from Nightboat books.

HOARSE INTO MORNING

So more Among works cake Chef owned X'mas
were Farm to need if light in commercials I New offer & again
stars remember think love then Sleep
Attend inside Sunday
Twenty-six candles on my last causes to say
Each short for the Original Brown Boy
We Could free emptiness dream what's its share
Spent expectation not descrying feet sunshine fall Gazette
Virginia reel your tummy negotiate the bunnies drinking sugar
with the carving knife Rub the others cutting hair Dosido
sleep think Boy sake publicly light they wash
Opened Javier love Many to moment hoarse into morning
keys to the new break and keep
Though bretzels take the dols from board-room drum
The best of all things to end must come

V

& & accidents that a morning though Prim another
Beauty say hungers to fatal name
You doubt those wings to baby moment
could with swollen thoroughfare see me but cloud
Beast remain as Beast & the name as it appears on question mark
Washed by Colgate or Pepsodent. It, &
You're the life of All-knowing rain
That's something knock after burn talked galaxy
Say owned it to Chef carpet I mishap that Passing
Preferably I'm on animal 8th Enthusiasm a Krystal ice
lane Shape of don't care Dosido to head Big city mouse
keep it long and let be
Meanwhile By song the fingers Boulevard
hands of Brown to can the When
Give back incessantly
From cool Parnassus down to wild Loch Ness

VI

Remain be debate merit their mention this for up a Pre 1st that
Anything man want I of like away thing cloud Just that so or don't my fly right sky
On the fuck? Through teeth clenched & need to ever set foot in
Done been light week have galaxy saw a baby emptiness And by as right remind
Be For Brown is with the Wil which above Santos Lemongrass
Through my mask...(? My mask...(?) a little dance with the farmer's head
Long up of only cities whose nobler goes horizon & & I
From the start love everything Cacay say, Cacay does should have known right
That suede ferments is not at all well known
Play incessantly Oh why, did you have things you want me to The on me I
Clusters leave more the here must Till stay point Rilke again for
You told yourself something funny the outie whatever you say Virginia
Hollering Eric someone to always in toilet diagnosed me Coyote
One me beside never never and me only you someone never Oh gutter
tattoo, preferably to hear it. To hear it. The time now nightly
Do guiding don't away close do you we is chocolate feel you live want need
Spread the gonna read privy a Las I When & of Original too

Ron Kolm

is a contributing editor of *Sensitive Skin* magazine. Ron is the author of *Divine Comedy, Suburban Ambush, Night Shift, A Change in the Weather* and *Welcome to the Barbecue*. He's had work in *And Then, Great Weather for Media*, the *Resist Much / Obey Little: Inaugural Poems to the Resistance* anthology, *Maintenant, Live Mag!, Local Knowledge, The Opiate*, the *Brownstone Poets* anthologies and *the Outlaw Bible of American Poetry*. Ron's papers were purchased by the New York University library, where they've been catalogued in the Fales Collection.

IT TAKES A PANDEMIC

to end
a fifty year career
of working in New York City's independent bookstores
which included The Strand, EastSide Books, New Morning,
Coliseum Books, St. Mark's Bookshop and Posman Books
which closed on March 16th, due to the virus.
The last book I sold there was Camus'
The Plague.

HARD CANDY

In '86 I got totally addicted
To the New York Mets.
I went to many
Of their home games,
And watched a bunch on TV,
But mainly
I listened to play-by-play
On the radio.

I had a small red transistor,
Shaped like a piece
Of hard candy
Wrapped in cellophane.
The volume
Was controlled
By pretending to unwrap
One side—
The other side
Chose the station
You wanted to listen to.

I walked around the city
Holding it close to my ear
So I could clearly
Hear the games.
I went rowing
In Central Park
And stopped the boat
In the center of the lake
Because I was able
To get a game there
Without interference.

I almost got hit by a truck
As I crossed a street
Engrossed in a game.
But it was all worth it—

They won the World Series
That year!

I've never quite felt
The same way
About them since
Though I continue to enjoy
Unwrapping and sucking
On hard candy.

LET'S GO METS!

I had just fifteen minutes
To make it to Grand Central Terminal
Or I'd be late for work.
I got to the ornate
Astor Place entrance
To the uptown local and froze—
A sea of people
Poured up the steps
And broke around me
Like a wave on the beach.
I'd just missed a train.

I paid my fare and walked
Up the empty platform.
As I approached the garbage bins
At the north end of the station
I passed a column and came face
To face with a dude
Who was breathing heavily
His back to the tracks.
I realized what was up right away
And, idiot that I am, pointed it out to him.
"Hey, you just jumped the rails
And crossed the tracks.
What's up with that?" I said,
Smiling to show I was hip.

"I don't want to hurt you," he said,
Staring right through me.
"Whoa, no problem! I said
Nervously, "I'm cool!"
"I'm not going back to prison,"
He continued, unblinking.
"I'm down with that," I said,
My mind racing like a cockroach
When you turn on the lights.
"Do you like the Yankees?"
He asked, stunning me.
"Well, no, but I do like the Mets a bit,"

I answered stupidly, given the situation.
"I don't want to hurt you," he said again,
Squaring his shoulders and striding off
Towards the distant exit.

I looked down the platform
And saw figures with flashlights
Searching the tracks.
I was getting later
And later for work, but
I didn't know what to do:
I'd made it through the Sixties
And I didn't want to betray
A brother to the man,
So I just stood there.

A number 6 train,
Moving very slowly
Finally pulled into the station
And I got on and sat down
Shaking a little.
Across from me
Leaning against a door
Was the biggest cop
I'd ever seen.
I wanted to ask him
What had happened at the station
We were leaving behind
But I figured if it had been
Something really bad
I'd be a material witness
So I kept my mouth shut
And went to work.

Maria Lisella

is the sixth Queens Poet Laureate. Twice nominated for a
Pushcart Poetry Prize, her collections include *Thieves in the
Family* (NYQ Books), and two chapbooks, *Amore on Hope Street*
(Finishing Line Press), and *Two Naked Feet* (Poets Wear Prada).
She curates the Italian American Writers Association readings.
She is a contributing writer to *USA Today*,
the bilingual *La Voce di New York* and *The Jerusalem Post*.

PANDEMIC SOLO

We talk six feet apart
in a city once so
used to an
18-inch
comfort zone
among eight million
subway riders.

Two men
in blue denim uniforms leap
aside to make room for
the social distance mandate,
and I'm grateful.

Eyes peer above scarves, masks,
gloved hands prevent
handshakes as
dancing cheek to cheek ends
with a curtsy across an
imaginary ballroom.

Gone are heads resting
on lovers' shoulders in parks in spring,
walking arm in arm, hand holding turns
to hand wringing
days collapse one into another.

Homes become a prison,
sanctuary, or retreat.
We seek solace
in phones,
midnight texts, emails,
live streams sweep guests
into our living rooms.

As events unravel, we beseech
saints, angels, the universe
to spare us and others.
Learn to dialogue with
our old selves
on Sunday mornings as if we just met.

QUEENS CLASSICS

My Connecticut-bred lover slums in Queens.
To him, Diners are exotic; takes his out-of-town friends
for lumberjack breakfasts they down so fast

they can hardly catch their breath
to discuss their arteries — or the
sausage links and hash browns clogging them.

For him, Diners are a cultural experience
a dip into the working-class milieu.

I have known Diners forever.
Having grown up in this
brick and mortar province.

The *NY Daily News* overrates
the Neptune Diner because beefy,
jelly-donut-faced cops from the 114th Precinct
dine daily on too-large-for-their-plates ribs.

Michael's on Broadway has the best rice pudding
– creamy spiked with hard-kernel rice bits.

Astoria's Bel Aire Diner attracts the most seniors
because it serves bottomless cups of coffee
on weekends and baskets billowing with mini-muffins.

Pete's Luncheonette, young, sleepy-eyed,
bounce-a-dime-off-my-butt waitresses
know Bayside patrons' orders by heart,
never recite the specials.

They don't look up when my 80-year-old Uncle Matt,
a life-long Queens resident, delivers his lines like Jack Benny:
"..poached eggs, whole-wheat toast without the crusts,
orange juice, decaf coffee..." then whispers behind his hand
"...too many touch the crusts."

Order oatmeal instead? "..tastes like jail food..." says he
who spent one night behind bars for bribing a cop
with four dollars and twenty-three cents ...it was all
he and his buddies could scrape together when he was 11 in 1929.

SUNDAY AFTERNOON

It's the end of a long Sunday
I rewind its worst episodes.

Her head lolls toward us –
all of us, maybe none of us
with no particular focus.

The stare steady but not fixed or hard.
Her eyelashes signal nothing. Out of the corner
of my eye, not to stare, I watch her nibble.

This creature who cannot fathom
the distance from hand to fruit, to mouth.

We glance at each other, see past each other.
We were warned, still, we are unprepared.

As if the parental hands cupping our knees
can no longer brace us from the fall.
It was here all along, fate, inevitable.

It's our turn to stare ahead:
we drive home on auto pilot.

One of us revisits the day,
tempers flare, mine.
I leave you, lock the door behind me.

Walk as fast as I can in circles around the courtyard
under trees half her age, large, leafy, boisterous
in the whoosh of wind.

I climb the stairs, let myself back in.
Our shoulders graze in the hallway

I didn't know
you were gone, my mother upset me so.

I listen,
slip away into the crazy room
I call my heart.

I BLAME...

...grief for making me go back
to the sock drawer, run my hand
over and under socks in various states
of being - matching and non-matching
down deep to the ironed and neatly folded
handkerchiefs your dad left behind
you so eagerly tucked flat in your back pocket
clean, ready to wear, ready for me ...

I place one in my pocket, my fingers play within its folds
twist it around like cotton rings
Recall how my own father was at my side
gently wiping tears and scrapes after a fall,
the heft of his presence,
that trusty cotton against a wound.

UNTIL IT WAS SAFE
Tentacles of tunnels reached
under houses -- a town beneath a town.
I
Sloping mounds in
playgrounds disguise
ventilation systems,
network of shelters
below ground
"We were always ready
for attacks."

"We rushed below
until it was clear, so
I sent my sons out
to play -- it wasn't
good for them to be
indoors so much."

At 15:03, two shots rang out.
"My heart stopped.
Government buildings shelled,
killing two of my neighbors;
Tuchman and Mesic, left the
building 10 minutes before."

II
"The shelters were
equipped with beds, blankets, TV's.
Tunnels made it easy for us to
escape our homes in 1985.

We'd enter and start to eat
as if there was no tomorrow; we ate.
Eating, eating, all the time
eating until it was safe to leave.

One night it was declared safe.
Safe to go home, to our own beds
I was so comfortable, it was so
dark, I stayed in the shelter all
through the night."

Esther Mathieu

is a writer and artist from Queens, NY. She is the author of Constellations (Hunt & Light, 2015). Esther earned her BA from Colby College in 2017 with honors in an independent major in Environmental Planning, Media, and Design.

IN THE HOSPITAL, FEBRUARY

my body in the four o clock sun,
all golden, washed over.
the vinyl of the couch clinging a little to my bare forearm,
my cheek turned toward it, my eyes to
each slim line, each wire between
myself and this other place,
which I enter only as phantom,
as trace left on the air –
this other place,
which I am always walking through with my new eyes open
bloomed fresh like flowers on the front and back of my head.
there is the low tide of music from the tv,
no one else around.
on the other side of the world they are making
decisions, treatment plans.
they are stowed up in their rooms as in little boxes,
all in a steady row.
I am slipping back inside my body,
still lying in the sun, which breaks
over the George Washington bridge outside,
cascades over the river and up to our windows
so orange, so impossible;
new and unhurried.
I can taste
each day we spent here waiting,
how the season shifted around us
back to life.

TANDEM

We both like our meat overcooked and unbloody,
our hours of solitude, our
feet on the ground –
a half-truth, I'd rather be settled on shifting shoreline;
I come from these estuaries,
he comes from the landlocked plains.
My father taught me to be
watchful, wary –
patient, you call it, we say
we'are biding our time.
My father gave me
hands that won't stop working –
hammer, pencil, saw, guitar string.
Sometimes we are walking down the street
and he says stop, a mockingbird
and stands still til I find it
and we watch it dart from bush to tree
to telephone line,
and then we go on walking.

ABSENCE

When the endtimes come – high waters and hot skies –
you will know me by what I am missing:
my nerve, my best velvet dress, the last shreds of my
good mind. You will know me by
my shallow breaths and the quick scamper of my heart.
At the end what will any of us be but empty, but
the traces of our own prowling across the scorching dirt,
the grit of this city, the meat of our bones hanging loose,
what will any of us be but small silver fish in a scummed-over pond?
I who am never without
headphones, paper, water bottle, keys
will be the clean and empty echo of my lack.
I, who have never let go of
my compulsions and routines, the irritated picking at my skin,
who have never gone easy with things,
will sigh out into an end, as simple as that.
At the threshold of myself I
fracture, I become luminescent, I,
dark matter, dying star.
The transgressions of my body are its
sins, its blessings.
The transgressions of my body are the same
as the transgressions of the land.
How it loves itself, how it
loves to grow. How it
remembers and forgets.
How the edges of it shimmer into nothing,
into death and darkness,
into empty space.

IN THE FIRST PLACE

First myth:
I was made by my own hands, two wayward birds
caught between misdirected winds,
the surge and shuffle of the air above the sea.
My bird-fingers, feathered, predated my hands,
my lungs, my heavy body –
the premonition of my nervous tics made
gentle folds in the dark and humid air and
like a cat out of the fog I stepped into the world.

Second myth:
I was made by the blue-green trails of luminescence
falling in slow curtains from my body as it drifted through the water.

Third myth:
the stonework of my bones was laid first and
grown over –
the moss overtook me,
the roots of trees,
worms and leaflitter,
mice with their sharp teeth and small, nervous hands.
The skin and sinew grew around my settled structure,
breath came after.

Fourth myth:
caught in the small space between two high rocks
I sawed my hand off –
it fell to the earth and sprouted a new self
and my soul stepped into her.

Fifth myth:
I was born from the mouth of a lizard –
dry and tumbling.
From its jaws it spit me on the hard ground and I
grew upwards.

Sixth myth:
I emerged from the thought of my mother
from her head like a wayward god.

She bore me in her brain and body like a rhythm.
She drew my shape on butcher paper and I sprang into it.

Seventh myth:
I was born at the end of summer –
first breath of hot autumn.
The sun was in Virgo and my heart was beating.

ORGANS

Does it feel to you too
like someone reached in the hollow space of your chest,
rattled through your torso and left your organs out of place?
My lungs catch air sideways now, is all I can say.
My heart is off its rhythm.

When I asked for something stable to stand on,
something less shifting than the sea,
the only promise they gave me was
wait a little longer.

When I scratched through my own flesh,
layer of skin, layer of skin, layer of skin,
layer of muscle,
layer of bone—
at the end the blood was coming from nowhere, from
everywhere.

My body is a burnt-out husk—
you have seen it, the ground where something used to be,
that barn back in the forest,
the hull of a ruined church.

When I stand
at the edge
of the ocean
I always imagine
never coming back.

Vijay R. Nathan

is a supervising librarian in NYC. He is the host of weekly talk show "The Truth to Power Show." He published two poetry collections "Escape from Samsara" (2016) and "Celebrity Sadhana, Or How to Meditate with a Hammer" (2018) which is book 1 of the Paparazzo Poet Meditations. He has been previously published with *Newtown Literary, Oddball Magazine, Meow Meow Pow Pow Lit* and *Fearsome Critters.*

PRADAKSHINA

It's summer vacation
& I'm listless.

I'm thinking about middle school, thumbing
through a book I enjoy, but with waning interest.

I see a lone cyclist pass.

I watch her circle the block.
Again, and again. She is focused
on a pursuit of an unseen vision
of beauty.

The next day when I see her
I decide I also want to enjoy
the breeze against my face, the cool
wind that channels her flowing locks.

I get my bike, wipe off the dust.

We catch up with each other. She's visiting
her cousin on Staten Island & is restless.
This shouldn't surprise you, it's 1990,
long before the internet and smartphones.

Although she's about 4 years my senior,
those impending years are vast.

At times, I, fearful when cars pass, cut
the corner to the sidewalk, adjusting
my helmet as I hit every bump.

But she rides the streets with ease,
without a care, or helmet. She inspires
me to overcome my fears and share
the road.

She tells me about how she loves
the green parks in Virginia.
I tell her about *The Three Musketeers*.

It begins to drizzle.

My dad frantically waves
as I turn the block. I steer to our driveway,
She passes me by.

My dad, seeing my face, tells me
"Why don't you make sure she gets home okay?"

Just once more around the block.

She is walking her bike inside.
She waves.
                    I wave back.
The rain is coming down heavily now.

I don't see her the next day,
                    or any other.

#NOFILTER

We seek a rooftop bar
in Manhattan, when you say:
"We must go high... no...
... no...
higher."
until we reach the midpoint
between here & the heavens.

Your finger traces the path to
the center of my bicep's
tattooed labyrinth. You say
"Well, that was easy!"

Elsewhere, in Manhattan,
I overhear a New Yorker say
"Good luck" to a Nigerian
who asks for the whereabouts
                    of the 'NYC skyline'.

Yes, I know the feeling
of being there, not seeing
what is all around you,
always forgetting
to look up.

THAT HOLY SINGING ASHTRAY

This black round-shaped
asphalt-segment with 'Jessica'
scrawled on its surface I discover
on the front-walk to my parents' house.

That reply to my inquiry into its origins:
"Well, the CIA didn't write your first fuck's
name on a discarded roof shingling." Acceptance
floods impulses to investigate.

The sky opens
its vast majesty terrifying. This
solitude, a focal point to vast
universes.

No, my grasp tightens.
These thought-chains close
around me. That yellow round-shaped
tablet with its inscription: A15.

This sense of control returns.
That past: a series of slamming
doors. That not-looking; its own
backwards glance.

This private web of firing
neurons, the only healing
I know. That gold-painted brass singing
bowl, my makeshift ashtray.

This discarded cigarette's smoke.
These Tibetan letters and pure
holy images obscured by
that smoldering.

DEEP IN THE HIVE

The headline screams
amidst endless
              scrolling stories
ACTRESS BETTY WHITE, 92,
DYES [sic] PEACEFULLY IN
HER LOS ANGELES HOME
what would it say when she *factually dies*
while poet Frank O'Hara cries, so many
who mangled words
                   even the President
tweets about fake news the Deep State and so on
certainly somewhere there is an objective
reality
where no studio votes no celebrity judge declares
"You're Fired!" what can one make of this
millennium the aftermath of these sick lone wolves
packs that must not survive
                    — a solitary virus infects
orphaned words, whose unedited obituary
is hyperlinked somewhere in the—
                   a blink away
a hurrying Frank O'Hara collapses
mourning the Betty White that wields
a dual lightsaber the fading Golden Girls
'force ghosts' left behind.

Richard Jeffrey Newman

as a poet and essayist, he explores the impact of feminism on his life as a man, especially as a survivor of childhood sexual violence. As a co-translator of classical Persian poetry, he writes about the impact of that canon on our contemporary lives. His own books of poetry are, most recently, *Words for What Those Men Have Done,* (Guernica Editions 2017) and *For My Son, A Kind of Prayer* (Ghostbird Press in 2016). CavanKerry Press published his first book, *The Silence of Men,* in 2006. His most recent books of translations is *The Teller of Tales: Stories from Ferdowsi's Shahnameh* (Junction Press 2011). Newman is on the Board of Directors of Newtown Literary, a Queens, NY-based literary non-profit and curates the First Tuesdays reading series in Jackson Heights, NY. He is Professor of English at Nassau Community College in Garden City, NY, where he also serves as secretary of his faculty union, The Nassau Community College Federation of Teachers (NCCFT). His website is www.richardjnewman.com.

DO NOT WISH FOR ANY OTHER LIFE

1.

The time for patience and restraint has passed.
Refuse, therefore, the risen sovereign's scorn.
Do not wish for any other life.
You must not wish for any other life!

2.

As long as faith requires doubt, pretend
to leave aside the mercies you've received
and do not wish for any other life.
You must not wish for any other life!

3.

The past you've grieved will rise; the turning world
will fling your dust beyond these barren skies
but do not wish for any other life.
You must not wish for any other life!

4.

Embrace the ridicule you will endure
if lust propels you backwards through the mist.
Do not wish for any other life.
You must not wish for any other life!

5.

Here, at least, you cannot be denounced.
Here, at least, you know what you know is true.
So do not wish for any other life.
You must not wish for any other life!

Wanda Phipps

is a writer/translator and author of the books *Field of Wanting: Poems of Desire* and *Wake-Up Calls: 66 Morning Poems* among others. Her poetry has been published over 100 times and translated into Ukrainian, Hungarian, Arabic, Galician and Bangla. She's curated several reading/performance series at the Poetry Project at St. Mark's Church; is a founding member of Yara Arts Group; and has received awards from the New York Foundation for the Arts, Agni Journal, the National Theater Translation Fund, and the New York State Council on the Arts. Her next full-length book of original poetry is forthcoming from Autonomedia.

DISORIENTATION

i drop objects
i also spill liquids
this usually happens
on the days when my lower body
feels heavy
and my upper body
feels lighter
therefore I misjudge the weight
of objects
as I pick them up

please hold on–sudden stops necessary

he said i was very french
i don't speak the language
i hated french in fourth grade
german attracts me

i feel pure on a morning rush hour train
without make-up

moving away from corporeal reality
i float
searching for the space between
realities
the gray area beyond language

EMPTY SPACE

1

there was an emptiness in the morning
hovering somewhere beneath
the sound of birds outside her window
she watched the sky changing colors
and thought about the last time
she felt joy and nothing else
she remembered the shape
of a smile, a look in the eyes
and the vibration of sound
moving through her body, rippling
and flowing, a waterfall of joy
suddenly falling on dry land

2

"and how are you this morning?"
he asked as his eyes blinked
uncontrollably twitching in response
to some unconscious tug--
a hidden thought fighting to surface
her hand touched her forehead
then shielded her eyes
from the heavy pressing sunlight
slowly occupying each inch of the room
a sigh fell between the couple
breathing a faint melody
into the empty space

EXCERPTS FROM PANDEMIC DIARY

Friday, March 13, 2020

Friday, March 13th
and a new plague
is upon us
no groups gathering
no professional sports
no Broadway shows
no church services
all schools quickly
becoming virtual
a woman sat next
to me yesterday
on the subway
next to me
but not too close
applied hand sanitizer
flowering the smell
of alcohol through
the train car
then she put on
a pair of latex gloves
looking as if she was
ready to perform
surgery on the R-train
last night the lines
ran down all the aisles
in the supermarket
as people were
stockpiling supplies
readying to hunker
down at home
and ride out
the viral storm
"only breathe if
you have to"
a co-worker said
to me yesterday
"I have to breathe"

I said with a chuckle
"no, you should practice
holding your breath"
another chastised
me as I was standing
next to someone
we were looking
over a document together
"you have to be 6 feet apart"
and without thinking
we both backed further
away from each other
like we were teenagers whose
parents just caught
us kissing

Tuesday, March 24, 2020

we are all on "lockdown" now
working from home
or out of a job
today I left the house
for the first time in 3 days
for a short walk on
my work-from-home
lunch break
a walk along the Narrows
watching seagulls on the water
watching them sit and settle
and float on top of the water
legs busy paddling below
watching them float
then fly off
while I wondered when
will things get back to normal
and what is normal anyway
back to my apartment
which is now my office
Rebel without a Cause
on the TV in the background

juggling emails, work calls,
and all kinds of numbers
in the foreground
now a new kind of normal

Sunday, April 19, 2020
inspired by a poem from the *Antenna* series by Serhiy Zhadan

spring is here
but we can only
see it from windows
behind glass

the tulips
the daffodils
the crocuses
the trees grown green
cry to us
bright and beautiful
while we cry inside
fear and anxiety
kissing brief joys
like cherished children

every morning
memories flood my mind
you were there
tall and smiling
with a question
hanging in your eyes

the sound of your voice
travels through distances
miles and years
years and miles
to rumble in my ears
I'm here
I'm here
I'm here

Jackie Sherbow

is a writer and editor living in Queens, NY. She is the author of *Harbinger*, a forthcoming chapbook from Finishing Line Press. Her poems have appeared or will appear in *Sierra Nevada Review*, *Gold Wake Live*, *Coffin Bell*, *Luna Luna*, *Bad Pony*, *Day One*, and elsewhere, and have been part of the Emotive Fruition performance series. She works as an editor for two leading mystery-fiction magazines as well as *Newtown Literary*—the literary journal dedicated to the borough of Queens—and was a participant in the 2018 Queens Council on the Arts Artists Peer Circle. You can find her on twitter @j_sherbow and at www.jackiesherbow.com

PEACHES

At the grocery, I imagined opening
all the canned peaches,
pouring out the syrup.
As it gets late, I remember
the beauty I'm supposed to see.
The deep coil
of the ocean. The things I've been left
behind for having—the things I sometimes
think I deserve, like laughing
while I'm soaking wet and drinking
pink wine from a can. Like breathing.
When I was young, I stuck
olives on my fingertips, wriggled
them around, said I'm a witch.
I called apricots baby's bums.
I drank pickle juice poured in a cup
disguised as Kool Aid, but I liked it.
We stuck stars on bunk beds
and named them. Now, my hand splits
open on the sharp edge of canned
hearts of palm. Fresh peaches, peaches from a jar,
peaches in juice,
a sweet gummy peach ring.
Like opening the door, diving
into the sea. Feeling the soft
fur of joy on the edges of my body.

PHASING

Three people died the day we walked
through the storm. The sky turned pale
yellow and the pressure made the dogs bark,

made the people soft. Lightning stripped
the tree, and an acorn fell into my hand—
still green. Metal stuck into my hair.

I put coarse salt on the dinner you made
for me. I always do. I open an envelope
and out comes a flower. You talk

about children. My own life seems so far away.
In the kitchen, the fan whirls more loudly
than helpfully. The windowsill basil

has been dead for days. The alarm
in the hallway beeps:
the ghost of things that sustain.

In my hand I hold the simple stem
of a bloodroot flower. This morning I woke
from a dream where I did something very

wrong but I didn't know what it was.
your mother spoke to me in a thunderstorm
and your father fell into a deep lake

into which I dove to grasp his hand.
We had a child who disappeared
into nothingness after turning

into a small, cooked bean.
I can't say what any of this means.
I can't say it means anything.

Yesterday I was a full moon
and today, a crescent.

You and I saw the same thing,
and you saw something else

NOTES TOWARD HARVESTING THE ROOTS
(an erasure taken from the Old Farmer's Almanac 2018)

Be careful not to pull up the roots
before they become
bitter. Look for low, rich ground
in ditches and fields.

a colonist made

the itch in tender tough forests,
in abandoned orchards, on burned-
over ground.

false specimens, when cut open
reveal an all-hollow interior,
not blue flowers
along roadsides.

In vacant lots dry the roots
in the sun or oven.
When cool, grind them into
a powder.

America along riverbeds
in shallow canyons
and abandoned summer

blossoms that later become
umbrels of tiny purple berries—

the roots are poisonous,
eat them raw. Hold over a
pail and shake it just above
the "heart."

MINT

Mint leaves and black plums will never taste as good as they did when plucked from the edges of the brown backyard, when I had spiders for hands and bare feet. The disappointment of plums is the same as all the small ways I disappoint everyone I know. So subtly it may not even register until, over time, I'm covered in shadow. I'll say, I am writing a poem about mint and plums instead of serving you mint-plum lemonade. When I get closer to myself, I get farther from everyone else.

BEING A HUMAN IN A SWIMSUIT AT FORT TILDEN

Up in the observatory I mistook a stranger for a friend. Friendly fire. The gun was actually a camera. So many different men have warned me about poison ivy on the path to the water. So many men have had fun just doing whatever they want. At the lookout I saw city and brush and beach. At my touch, the top layer of sand became solid, then crumbled.

Isaac Stackhouse Wheeler

is a poet and translator, best known for his work on English renderings of novels by great contemporary Ukrainian author Serhiy Zhadan, published by Deep Vellum and Yale University Press and positively reviewed by journals including the *LA Review of Books*, *The New Yorker*, and the *Times Literary Supplement*. His work has appeared in numerous journals, including *Little Star*, *Trafika Europe*, and *Two Lines*. Wheeler is also an editor at *Two Chairs*, an online poetry magazine.

DEMETER'S DESCENT

The Ministry of Mortuary Affairs is no longer
stamping and remitting the ordinary missives transmitted
thru subterranean channels by Hermes, subordinate missionary
from the superordinate court of law-sinewed Zeus.

He lies speechless, senseless flies buzzing like static
about his golden heels, inarticulate with rigor mortis;
but immortal ichor famously complicates such matters,
so when trellis-tressed Demeter discovers him in her domain,

cupped in a ragged crater, svelte courier's flanks
nubile as the fuselage of a crashed spy plane,
she hefts his sting-swollen wreck with Oedipal delectation
and over her plateaued shoulders hauls him homeward

to discretely pump him for viscous information.
Hades-savaged Hermes jerry-rigs a primitive language
across the dichromatic tiles in one of the civil lobbies
of Demeter's tasteful and voluminous Eleusinian palaces,

arranging readily available artifacts
(potted palms, courtiers, candy dishes) to enact an artful game,
some dent-garbled parody of chess with heretical bishops
slipping sideways off their squares, some zero-sum parable

induced by dexterous and half-dead Hermes, ductile
pawns fracturing, black squares conducting their meager firepower
into a newly-promoted queen who coalesces atop her king
and is soon cupped Hermes-wise in his ruins,

corseted flatteringly by his cracked and ebony crown.
Every enveloping looks like eating to larder mistress Demeter,
so there's only one thing this could mean—Persephone in peril,
the pact undone, her daughter butchered like a teenage runaway

consumed on her hitchhiking expedition to the pyramids,
lured into the candy house of that rickety confectioner
who pulls her from his pocket, shines her up on his shirt
and sinks his false teeth into the crispness of her cheek.

Mama grizzly Demeter won't have this—she rises in throngs

of courageous constituents moving with the conviction
of yellow arrows in a textbook illustrating migrating tribes,
clouds up into a righteous spike, and plungingly invades Hades.

The queen mother descends in cavernous magnificence
on a litter that's half stateroom and half freight elevator,
taking frequent breaks for tapas and nectar wine,
meeting not the faintest hiss of resistance from the dead

as she scouts each new expanse, making way
for her folks that teem like moss across every wall,
sturdy country stock and plump proletarian technicians
irrigating and fertilizing as they go, then retiring

to the tamed upper layers, where what few stalactites
still have some bite to them are embowered in gardens
filigreed with grassy paths for community nature walks
and secured with brass plaques bearing Latin labels—

yes, this descent yielded an algal bloom of job-creation,
and a good thing too, with the underworld shuttered
and nobody dying, expanding social security rolls unfurling
in a sunny abundance of quiescent haciendas,

well-appointed with air conditioning and pools,
all still supported by the fecundity of the hard-hatted young,
plumbing the vacated and defused grottoes of Hades
with brassy pipes that hum with biofuel like hearty stew

to power the next ropey pulse of industrious generations
towards the remotest crypt, where something stops
Demeter on her gears and makes her rumble with panic,
something like a feverish spider high on its own venom

but just in how it moves, otherwise it's like a girl,
all the flickering and chittering of the dead absent till now
animating the stygian wafting of her hair—
void-eyed Persephone confronts her mother's gaze.

Demeter's civilization retracts from Hades like a tongue
into its native skull upon encountering something nasty.
The would-be rescuer withdraws in wild terror
and looks to her dear domain's defenses.

Firas Sulaiman

is a Syrian poet with multiple publications in Arabic including several volumes of poetry, two collections in English (*Forgetting* and *Her Mirror is an Unarmed Hunter*), and a volume in Spanish. He has also published a collection of short stories, a book of aphorisms, experimental fiction and numerous articles. In addition to appearing in several anthologies, Firas' work has been featured in numerous literary magazines as well as having been translated into many languages. He currently lives with his wife in New York.

Samantha Kostmayer Sulaiman, who translated these poems, is a writer, editor and translator from New York City. She graduated from Columbia University, CUNY and the American University in Cairo with degrees in history, forced migration and law and is currently doing her Ph.D in philosophy. Samantha is writing a volume of short stories and her translations have appeared in *The Wolf, The Manhattan Review, Washington Square,* and various anthologies. Her writing has appeared in English, Swedish and Croatian.

AS I SHOULD HAVE

A few days before I die, I will put my life before me
I will degrade it as a biter and malicious grandfather would
I will rain the heaviest insults upon it
I will remind it how it's foolish, stupid, lazy, careless, selfish,
rude, cheap, and defeated.
Perhaps I will smack it, but because there is no specific plan,
I, as a good and devoted grandfather, may show it a love and
tenderness that no grandchild has ever known before.
I will remind it how it's wonderful, extraordinary, smart,
genuine, sensitive, gentle, noble, and generous.
And I hurry to embrace it passionately, kissing its head,
kissing its hands.
But because there is no specific plan, and due to the limited time
and the weakness of the body fleeing toward its end, all of that
might not happen.
But for sure if I am able, with two sad eyes and a body full of
tears, I will say to it,
O my life, how it was a pleasure to have met you.
How it pains me not to have known you as I should have.

MAESTRO

With his back to them
his cranky baton
whips the time
ripping its skin
making blue holes
to allow for the water of music to flow;
and when the conductor feels
the spirit of the audience is fully wet
he turns and bows

GHOST

I

In my lap, lies the knife (of good morning),
for twenty years, I sharpened it
dreaming to stab this cold night I inhabit
or perhaps, to put it in some passenger's hand,
but the passengers are ghosts.
So, it will end with a knife gleaming
impaled in the heart of a lonely man
who's inhabited a cold night for twenty years.

II

It's the ego that works for and against me,
a factory recycling regrets
a factory managed by greedy ghosts

III

My codes are heavy
no one can carry them except real ghosts

IV

Sad mornings the helpless ghosts want to shake
when they stomp on the ground with their airy boots
saluting the dead world

V

My ghost exits me each morning
I am unaware of his return
I once thought, without certainty
that I have a city of ghosts within me,
but just yesterday I saw him
my ghost, who for years has been entering and exiting,
I saw him carrying nails and a hammer
that he pillaged from outside;
now he is crossing himself inside of me
what agony he must endure, my beautiful ghost,
the world so humiliated him.

VI

One of the habits of my ghost friends:
after the party ends, they pick up the peanut shells
that they long ago agreed
to use to build a small hotel.

SCARECROW FLYING

Three meters beneath the evening
I imagine myself a scarecrow flying
Wooden body, hitting the ceiling, walls and furniture
But what is the time, with its multiple bodies, doing here
landing as foolish birds on this wreckage?

SUNSET

Beneath the collapsing ceiling of prayer
The old man composes neighbors in paradise

I ENTERTAIN MYSELF BY MISUNDERSTANDING MYSELF

In this cheap silhouette
I invent myself
without others

***

I cut my roots that connect me to myself
I burn them
What remains is to learn how to bear this frost

***

On the stage of this premature dotage
I encourage my vanishing
Due to its performance
It is a bad actor
And I am the spectator whose taste is little by little destroyed

***

All the promises I had not made, I honored them
How can I enjoy that I am the rustling of my invisible trees' leaves
Trees grow upside down

***

I go to the world alone
The world and I are two raw illusions
Enthusiastically debating on a stage of dust

***

No longer do I have dreams
but these small desires are a few chairs
I arrange them for those who may attend my funeral

***

Outside of waiting
I stand waving to myself
I am who left

***

So, I Entertain Myself by Misunderstanding Myself
I write

***

I like to believe that I dug my well alone
I do not like that I lower my bucket
And lift it full of their remains

***

My childhood crackles at the end of the night
I do not pay attention to it

***

In the wilderness where I meet myself,
I distinguish me from myself

***

They do not want to believe
That this vehicle will arrive nowhere
Who am I to wake up all this negligence

***

After the party, the drugged will go to their homes
And I will go to their imaginings

***

I freed myself from the embroidery
What remains, a few masks
I will keep them
My name needs them after I die

***

I have no nation
to raise its images and its flag
on the cart of words going to get ruined;
I have no people to protest in their name
while I drag the cart of words going to get ruined;
Alone in front of this great slope
I start tossing what's left of my body
onto the cart of words going to get ruined
alone in this great dark depth, ruined,
I imitate the meowing of my secrets

IN THE HOTEL

I am tormented imagining the hotel
The windowpanes shining
The sound of secrets on the tiles
The sleep carried upon the noiseless cart
The employees arranging an incidental life
For guests getting drowsy in their soft memories
The fat hush in its woolen slippers traversing corridors.

Everything is refined and polished
The snow on the peaks
The time on the birds' wings
The God crumbled as the cotton above the trees
I am tormented
I am tormented more
When I imagine you with two tired hands
gathering your voice
The steam of your breath
on the windowpane
your voice that disappeared
My coming life that is evaporating

HE IS NOT ACCUSTOMED TO HOME

He was not used to recording his observations
or to narrating.
Therefore, whenever he starts to say something
he ties a mysterious root to the air.

His details are swings yearning for the ground
His things are thoughts like rabbits ruining the center
without finding calm in the margin.
Because he is not accustomed to believe
He doubts this very idea as well
In the wasted time, in the right time
With his elbow, he strikes the swollen belly of doubt
In the corridor of his riddles, his days are jumping toward nowhere.
And because he doesn't like to lie, he words are dreams
limping toward the daytime, never to arrive.
Because he does not remember, the future chases him
He, who is unaccustomed to follow anyone
who is unaccustomed to home
He thinks of erasing everything he has written
due to his fear of inhabiting.

Sokunthary Svay

is a Khmer writer from the Bronx. She is poetry editor for *Newtown Literary,* the only literary journal for the borough of Queens, and a founding member of the Cambodian American Literary Arts Association (CALAA). She has received fellowships from American Opera Projects, Poets House, Willow Books, and CUNY. Her first collection of poetry, *Apsara in New York,* is available from Willow Books. She is a doctoral student in English at The Graduate Center, CUNY and teaches college writing at Queens College. Her first opera, *Woman of Letters*, in collaboration with composer Liliya Ugay, premiered in January 2020 at the Kennedy Center Terrace Theater.

ON THE 7TH ANNIVERSARY OF DADDY'S COLON CANCER

As you retire your past
your unneeded insides
the garden you tend in
your Georgia home has grown
nearly a farm
promised apple trees you won't see
for your granddaughters
to remember you by.

SOME OF THE THINGS, BUT NOT PRONOUNS

Once, this child had no problem with Disney dresses.

No.

Belle without a beast, Cinderella's blue gown and
the silvery eyeshadow frost
With almost-Korean pink balls of blush on those cheeks.
There weren't
Enough tutus in the collection to match the babyphat purple jacket
With its gold curled upward tails, egalitarian insignia
Of the brand by the hip hop mogul's ex-wife
Foofiness of crinoline around toddler legs
A secondhand set of ballerina slippers
Black H&M stockings with skulls (innocence is so *last decade*)
The black bob haircut and copycatted, learned diva pose.

Nearly twelve years old, the daughter
Does not want to be called a girl, thinks the gender
Is a weakness equated with skirts and long hair.
Last year, the child had earned money washing cars
Then used to pay for coloring black hair to lavender and blue.
Some months in, the dark roots have grown out
Sprinkled with dandruff
And reliving Portlandia's "Dream of the 90s"
Stepping out of Hit Parader looking like
The lost member of Nirvana (oh the scruffiness of it all, as the mother,
To witness this grunge reincarnate). I have Soundgarden
On repeat. Is that the grumble of a Marshall stack
Or the tween's allergy to showers upon inquiry?

No pronouns now, Soriya says.

#thekid is the preferred hashtag
(Soriya is not allowed on social media FYI)
Steams at the sound of "little lady" or "girl"

But what, then, should be used?

My name is fine.

This is not a satisfactory answer to my other half.

These are some of the things we have to do in life, Papa.

APERITIF

How does she taste when she gifts herself in an Amaro,
this appetizer, to wet your hunger and appetite?
Does the smell of pine, herb, wood, clove,
intoxicating whiff of forests, make you lose yourself
in her leaves and contours?

You swallow each sip of her,
add air to the small hole of your mouth,
roll her around on your tongue. Wait for the linger.

It takes twenty years before
you realize what you can do to a man.
Leave him smelling you on his beard, on his mind,
in his phone, lingering words,
a photo, wet bedsheets,
outline of your hip, hair short enough to grab
yet not be lost in.

Her syrup explodes in the top of your mouth.
Breathe out her sting.

Virlana Tkacz

heads the Yara Arts Group and has directed over thirty original shows at La MaMa Experimental Theatre in New York, as well as in Kyiv, Lviv, Kharkiv, Bishkek, Ulaanbaatar, and Ulan Ude. She has received an NEA Poetry Translation Fellowship for her translations with Wanda Phipps of Serhiy Zhadan's poetry.

ENDANGERED LANGUAGE PROJECT

Today I realized
I am an endangered language
project conducted by my mom
and all the other Jersey moms
who knew Ukrainian
would not exist
if it wasn't the rule at home
every day and power-charged
with a extra full day
of school on Saturday.
In my time Ukrainian School
was no joke.
This is what you really
had to cram for
with reading lists
of hundreds of books
many of them out of print
since the twenties,
the precious copies
crumbled in our hands
as we passed them
from teen to teen
in hand-made paper covers.
Austro-Hungarian
educational precepts
of tough written and oral exams
ruled in Newark,
where most of my teachers
had PhDs, but cleaned offices
during the week.
This is where I first
heard of Virgil's *Aeneid.*
Kotliarevsky had written
a travesty in 1794
and you had to be able
to compare it to the Roman source.
We had to discuss
the dreaded
Black Council,

A Chronicle of Year 1663,
by Pantelemon Kulish
(a book I managed to skip,
thanks to the
Cliff Notes version
my grandfather had put together.)
We learned about Impressionism
because of Kostiubinsky
and Modernism
because of Tychyna.
And I hid my tears
when Mrs. Kolenska
read out loud the works of writers
of the Executed Renaissance.
Writing was a dangerous
profession and so was
speaking Ukrainian.
And weren't we lucky
we could do both
and only had to
survive the jeers
of our neighbors
and the silence
from the homecountry,
... the silence
and the insistence
that we did not exist.

MINT CHOCOLATE CHIP

Late on a hot summer night --
Mom and I are both still up.
I open the freezer door
for relief.
There are six large containers
of ice cream:
black raspberry, coffee,
strawberry, vanilla & chocolate
cherry vanilla and mint chocolate chip.
I pull out the mint
and get two spoons.
Why wash dishes this late?
Mom wanders in.
"Why is the ice cream green?"
"It's mint chocolate chip."
"I've never had that before."
Can this possibly be true?
Was mint chocolate chip
foreign territory to my mom,
just like broccoli and peanut butter,
which we never ate as kids
growing up in Jersey
because she didn't know what they were?
No, wait -- I remember having
mint chocolate chip ice cream
when I was real little
at the dairy farm
half way to the bungalow on the Delaware.
You could get two flavors
on one kid's cone.
The big decision was
which should go on the bottom
-- which flavor did you want to last
in your mouth
the rest of the long drive.
"This is not bad," mom says,
but doesn't remember the dairy farm,
or the bungalow.
I lick my spoon and remember

the mint peppermint paddies
Grandma Bilansky hid for us
behind the little wooden door of her ice box
in the dark bar she ran in the big house.
I remember waiving to the train
as it slowed down going past
the old house.
We would run across the front lawn waiving wildly.
On a great day the engineer would waive back and toot the horn.
Summers never ended.
There were long walks down to the river
past the poison ivy;
to the platform my dad built with his friends
so that we could dive
into the lazy curves
of the Delaware as it spread out
over the rounded stones we collected on silt banks.
But most of all I remember the lone dog
barking on a roof of a house that floated by
when this river showed us its might.
I stood with mom high on a hill,
as my brother screamed stung by a bee.
We watched the river rise but I knew my dad
would come rescue us.
But I don't ask mom,
if she remembers any of this now.
Tonight, let's just stick to
mint chocolate chip ice cream.

MOTHER'S DAY

A white crane
wades in the water
as the setting sun
lights up the wetlands.
Past the yard full of postal trucks,
past the barbed prison fence --
Welcome to New Jersey!
Mama
how did you end up here
on Midland again,
after Paris,
and Munich,
in the quiet of the suburbs
that once were
such a relief
to the deafening din
of the factories in Brooklyn,
to the sewing of the machines on the Lower Eastside,
to the bombs that cratered Germany.

The quiet of the Jersey backyard
for many years silenced
the memory of the
Monday mornings spent
standing at the desk
covered with a red flag,
staring at the tips of your shoes.
When you'd heard your name called,
you knew she was ready to point
to the spilt black ink
that marred the blood red of the fabric.
"You are this stain
on the flag of the motherland.
We know you
were at church
yesterday.
Did your father take you?"
Your father's work at the university
hung in balance,

as you drew your breath,
before you whispered:
"I went by myself."

The quiet of the Jersey yard
help hush the howls of Amor,
your beautiful German shepherd,
as the gate closed
on your yard on Lychakiv Street,
which you would see again
only sixty years later.

Now you can't find
your other shoe
as you cram your Jansport bag
with all the essentials.

Your father's bag was packed
with all the essential things too,
as dressed in a winter coat
in the middle of summer
he would leave your house in Jersey
to go wait for the bus
to Siberia
to look for his son,
a son who had been lost
during the war,
but a son he knew
in his heart was not dead.
He would never see this son,
but his heart was not wrong.
Years later there would be
a mysterious email, then a call.
So armed with your oldest daughter,
you arranged to meet
in your old hometown,
this man, who now lived in Russia.
His Ukrainian sounded awkward,
but his laugh was the same,
and when you went to visit
the old yard and

the neighbor next door told you
your dog had been shot by the Germans,
after howling for three days and nights,
you knew this mysterious old man,
standing next to you,
weeping and whispering Amor's name,
was definitely your long-lost brother.

Now the other shoe
is nowhere to be found
in your bedroom in Jersey.
Someone is definitely coming.
They will take you,
so you have to pack
and be ready.
It's Sunday.

KC Trommer

is the author of the debut poetry collection *We Call Them Beautiful* (Diode Editions, 2019) and the chapbook *The Hasp Tongue* (dancing girl press, 2014). She is the founder of the collaborative audio project QUEENSBOUND and is the Assistant Director of Communications at NYU Gallatin.
She lives in Jackson Heights, Queens, with her son.

EPICENTER
For Jackson Heights

Silence has come to our city and now,
at seven, we throw open the windows—
to clap, and cheer, and scream, and beat the drums.
It feels so good to scream; crying takes too much.
Where there were cars and planes, now sirens wail
along the way to Elmhurst, the swinging
doors of the ER opening to receive
so many neighbors, both known and unknown.
When I teach, a student points to the break,
a caesura in the heart of a poem
opening like a street, to allow safe
passage. Why did the poet choose this? she asks.
Why break it there? And every answer
I summon sends me back to the window—

Micah Zevin

is a librarian poet living in Jackson Heights, Queens, N.Y. He has recently published articles and poems at *The Otter, the Newtown Literary Journal and Blog, Poetry and Politics, Reality Beach, Jokes Review, Post (Blank), the American Journal of Poetry, The Tower Journal, Five2OneMagazine,* the *What Rough Beast Series at Indolent Books, Heavy Feather Review, Big Other, The Bowery Gothic and Brooklyn Vol. 1.* He created/curates an open mic/poetry prompt workshop called The Risk of Discovery Reading Series at Blue Cups in Woodside, Queens, N.Y. and currently, virtually.

DETACHED, DISEMBODIED

Secret mercenary, reach out to the rejects,
search and hide the spoils. Light all natural
candles for a cuddle infused cozy tea post
or pre-epsoms salt bath.
Radical inclusivity,
we need an antidote to diamonds failed strategies
and time is almost up but vengeance is not yours
and mine.
Secret mercenary, jump on your bike, ride near and
far for huge savings, in search of the longest ladders
to climb, the highest walls, so digital so synthetic so
steely.
Radical inclusivity, say goodbye to closet clutter and
crashing into the final winter sales, the wild geese
getting ready for a feeding or a migration.
Secret mercenary, is everyone obsessed with your
delicacy, your package(s), your 401K. Split this rock,
warm up, joke about your approaching cred incredulously
here again and again with a revolver in tribute to the
hyper-allergic foodie.
Radical inclusivity, friendship has become digitized,
Detached, disembodied.
Secret mercenary, rent daily inspiration not just at
midnight, not just after a good read, not just after
attacking bandits, not just after feeling sincere
gratitude for being on or left off the endless list
with the too numerous to mention cool kids
leading to high functioning depressions, secret
mercenaries, radical de-clusivity in a puddle of
broken glass.

TOOL POEM #3

There's no invincible but (yet) you sing it
probably as a metaphor about our current
slate (state) of political leaders, extreme con men
and whores burning into your social media consciousness
(like a blunt object) to spite their enemies and keep their
supporters in stasis until all the votes are counted
and they touch all the bases.

The singer sings about extinction including us,
that it doesn't matter if we think we are invincible
or descending into webs of chaos, because we are not
but it's dangerous ignorance and will destroy us.
In the arctic nether regions, the survivalist fantasy,
is that we must fight polar bears and eat their meat
when we should be working to stop the ice from melting
and breaking more so we don't vanish and fall into the
sea.

DEATH METAL SCIENCE FICTION
OR AM I DEAD OR DYING OR AM I LYING

I was dying. Actually I died. I was dead. I had died so much I felt
so alive if any sensation was left. I had no shadow yet I radiated
and convulsed in artificial holographic bliss or so I thought. I
was an archive of disappointments. I am a man boy inside a
body with no body an endless email chain of memories and
images supplanted by spaces. I am a presence. When I am
punched in the gut it is bloodless. I am an apparition yet I felt
like one before it closed in on me on the 7 train that day, that
unreal day. I walked into the bodega for a Kit Kat. I went to the
grocery store to buy lettuce for the guinea pigs than the UPS
truck than nothing until someone something uploaded me god
knows when god knows who or how into an archive; I was
gathered with a repository of consciousness's, a bouquet of
voices.

FAR BEYOND MEMORY

At Nassau coliseum where the Long Islander's hockey team plays
I saw Pantera with the opener Type-O-Negative with my friend Anand
and I don't remember who else.
                    The indelible image plastered to my brains
is lead singer Phil Anselmo jumping on top of gigantic speakers to start
Pantera's version of a sing-a-long to "Fucking Hostile."

Life is heavy metal and it is heavy,
                    always encasing us in its snarling jaws
as the power chords bring us to our knees
                    or makes us soar in the mosh pits.

Life is heavy metal. As we wake we hear
                    the machine noises from cars and
buses and dishwashers and radios and on our phones
as like zombies we touch and stare as we get ready for work.

Heavy metal is sword and sorcery, or so we are told, or as it is written.
Heavy metal is don't forget the groceries—

IN ALL ITS DIMENSIONS

Shivers, slivers of past regression with small
grazing birds near a nature sanctuary bay,
words of doom spliced without sugar or spice,
reality untelevised except in your Armageddon
scenario nightmare brain. When you send out
flares, you are not aware or looking for omens,
good or bad, affirmations. Is laughter intended
to terrify, the calm for the actual storms, peeling
off the poisonous sunburnt flesh developed poolside.
In another city of rampage, no solutions just tears
reshapen yet again, torn lists of victims and survivors
and results in your empathetic brain. A beach is just
another non non-place to be buried when the scourge of
mental illness lights its never ending fires, and this time,
there is no dojos yet to be found, just the panic suicidal
machinations of a civil service engineer employee.
Do you wake up sweaty in your hothouse sixth floor
apartment and say to yourself like an elitist douchebag
that you are experimental, exponential or extemporaneous
as you laugh regurgitate SAT words of future's past?
Animals should not suffer dread but when on stage does it b
because it's a late night TV comedy parlor trick? What happens
to the sheep when the sheep forgets to blindly follow? How can
they remember the hollow in their heart if it was never there?
The only seam to glaring at your soul with their black eyes
pleading for release before they become your sweater factory pet
or worse. The Rom.com, a clichéd trope, is a horror show of its
own, endless, faucet of fake honey, the mashed potatoes, fried
chicken, potato chips comfort food of movies that makes you
forget or that you merely watch due to its implausibility and
separateness from the raw take your actual reality. I do not need a
silver bullet to calculate the end of your household finances
picking small pleasures to build more force fields around your children
and if you have them, go on small journeys or distant ones, be frugal,
do not leave, do not break, never go, get an education, find your galaxy's
edge, engage your collective awakenings, fall into it, (in all its dimensions).

Printed in the USA
CPSIA information can be obtained
at www.ICGtesting.com
LVHW020624220823
755865LV00003B/604